How To Have More Courage

I0482294

HTeBooks

Disclaimer

This book is designed to provide condensed information. It is not intended to reprint all the information that is otherwise available, but instead to complement, amplify and supplement other texts. You are urged to read all the available material, learn as much as possible and tailor the information to your individual needs.

Every effort has been made to make this book as complete and as accurate as possible. However, there may be mistakes, both typographical and in content. Therefore, this text should be used only as a general guide and not as the ultimate source of information. The purpose of this book is to educate.

The author or the publisher shall have neither liability nor responsibility to any person or entity with respect to any loss or damage caused, or alleged to have been caused, directly or indirectly, by the information contained in this book.

Table of Contents

How Will This Book Help You?

This book aims to help build courage in all the aspects of one's life—physically, emotionally, morally, and intellectually by acknowledging fear at its source and eventually overcoming it through understanding.

"Courage is resistance to fear, mastery of fear—not absence of fear. Courage is not the lack of fear. It is acting in spite of it."

– Mark Twain

Acknowledging Fear as the Source of Courage

"Fear is essential for courage."

– John F. Murray

Since courage is simply defined as a person's willingness and ability to ultimately take action despite his fear of different things, the basic presumption is that courage requires fear in order to be exercised. It involves the existence of costs, risks, or at least a conceived threat resulting from one's action where one's ability to act in spite of them renders his act as courageous. Therefore, without fear, there can be no courage.

What is fear?

Fear is the personal sensitivity of an individual towards any harmful threat to any aspect of his well-being. It is accompanied by the physical response of avoidance associated with stress and discomfort. Thus, it can be experienced in varying degrees depending on one's ability to escape the danger he is facing. For instance, mild fear is accompanied merely by a slight degree of nervousness; sensible fear is accompanied by distress, and intense fear is accompanied by alarm and panic.

A Closer Look at Fear: The Two Faces of Fear

How fear affects a person's life depends on how he looks at it. Fear has two faces: an agent for survival or a catalyst of death.

Fear as an Agent for Survival

Through the years, fear has enabled man to contribute many inventions that played a part in human survival and development. For instance, the fear of dying from dreaded diseases such as small pox contributed to the invention and discovery of vaccines and medicines. The fear of becoming extinct from extreme weather conditions has led to the invention of stronger residential structures and appliances such as heaters and air conditioning systems in order to cope with such changes.

In these cases, man's courageousness in bringing forth ideas and discoveries which were otherwise considered eccentric or even unacceptable at that time enabled his emancipation from the dominance of nature and allowed him to ultimately conquer his fear of death.

Fear as a Catalyst of Death

On the other hand, it is when one is unable to exercise courage that he suffers from either making rash decisions or mere inaction which causes psychological illnesses such as anxiety disorders and other related ailments that may lead to deterioration in health and ultimately, death.

In fact, data from the National Institute of Mental Health indicate that nearly twenty million individuals have been found to experience such disorders the United States alone. These mental illnesses often have detrimental effects on individuals and have been found to adversely affect their work, interpersonal relationships, and their personal coping mechanisms as well. Some have been found to develop aggressive behavior and destructive routines such as drug dependency, alcoholism, and other forms of hurtful practices including murder and suicide.

It is a matter of choice.

How fear affects one's life is a matter of choice.

Identifying One's Fear

"The weeds keep multiplying in our garden, which is our mind ruled by fear. Rip them out and call them by name."

– Sylvia Browne

Individuals often make inappropriate choices in life because they allow fear to cloud their minds. In order to have a clear mind, one must first learn to identify his fear. In general, there are three types of fear: physical, emotional, and psychological fear.

Physical Fear

Physical fear is the fear of matter that is concrete or that produce tangible effects. These include fear of living things like animals, insects, fellow humans, diseases, physical pain, loss of freedom and loss or destruction of properties. It is usually felt only when one encounters the subject of fear.

Many individuals usually fear animals which are wild, violent, or poisonous like jungle animals, snakes, scorpions, and spiders. They also fear fellow humans who appear aggressive or overwhelming. In terms of diseases, they often fear illnesses which are contagious, fatal, disfiguring, or repulsive such as measles, cancer, leprosy, and other infectious skin disorders. Physical pain includes pain from violent attacks or medical procedures such as bodily injuries, incisions from surgical procedures, blood extraction, and invasive laboratory procedures. Loss of freedom is likewise a physical fear because it can be manifested in one's inability to decide, act, or move on his own such as when he enters into a relationship or engages in illegal activities which warrant imprisonment.

Emotional Fear

Emotional fear is the effect of any event that causes emotional stress or pain such as rejection, failure, loneliness, ridicule or criticism, misery, and grief. They may be induced by events like such as being turned down from a marriage proposal, losing in a competition, undergoing a financial crisis, or losing a loved one through death or separation. These fears often hinder one from advancing or moving on with his life and sometimes prevents him from taking opportunities which are otherwise good for him.

Psychological Fear

Psychological fear refers to fears created in the mind. Since the human intellect is capable of recognizing the effect of certain situations in less than seconds, fear is triggered when one does not have any experience of a circumstance he currently faces. This is because the mind cannot identify the significance of the event with respect to the effects it may produce as he has no knowledge of such in his memory. This can be also called fear of the unknown.

Recognizing the significance of certain situations enables the mind to decide or act appropriately. In other words, it allows him to exercise some degree of control. Lessening one's ability to exercise control or to at least know what he must do in specific situations trigger fear.

As soon as one identifies his fear, he can then proceed to analyze the level of fear he has. Otherwise, all these types of fear may develop into phobias if not handled appropriately.

Fear clouds the mind. Having a clear mind requires getting rid of one's fears and ridding oneself of any fears is possible only if one knows what they are.

Analyzing One's Level of Fear

"Courage is a special kind of knowledge: the knowledge of how to fear what ought to be feared and how not to fear what ought not to be feared."

– David Ben-Gurion

It is normal for a person to have a rational fear of something. On the contrary, being fearless is dangerous as one may think that he is invincible and live without necessary precautions.

Not all fears are unreasonable. Only those which have the tendency to turn into phobias can be detrimental to one's life. Thus, it is unnecessary to put a strain on one's well-being by excessive worrying about the absence of courage except in cases where the danger of fear turning into a phobia is involved. It is therefore important to distinguish between the two levels of fear: normal fears and phobias.

Normal Fears

Normal fears include childhood fears which may be outgrown such as fear of the dark and monsters, and things or events which pose real threats to one's life. Some examples of things or events which pose as real threats to one's life are crime situations such as robberies, hostage-taking, kidnapping, and murder or simply being attacked while walking down the street at night.

Normal fears do not need to be addressed with courage since they can either be outgrown or resolved without resorting to courageous acts because the individual will have a means of responding to it. For instance, the fear of darkness is always solved by providing a source of light, while the fear of crime situations can be tackled using defensive tools such as blunt weapons, guns, or sprays.

Phobias

Phobias, on the other hand, are defined as unwarranted reactions of fear towards something that is not even present or imminent. The difference between normal fears and phobias are that normal fears occur at the time when one is faced with the object of fear while phobias do not grant the individual any room for preparedness because of the lack of imminence of the object feared. Instead, phobias create a wide-ranging fear accompanied by feelings of extreme dread and panic towards the certain object or situation such that one deliberately prevents himself from encountering them even if it inhibits him from his personal advancement or induces him to change his entire lifestyle.

According to data from the National Institute of Mental Health, more than ten percent or six million Americans in the last decade experience phobias. Some of the more common phobias are animal phobias such as fear of spiders (arachnophobia), snakes (ophidiophobia), reptiles (herpetophobia), and birds (ornithophobia); situational phobias which pertain to specific events such as flying (aerophobia), climbing heights (acrophobia), being in places where one feels they cannot escape (agoraphobia), or being in enclosed spaces (claustrophobia); medical phobias which include fear of medical professionals themselves such as fear of doctors (iatrophobia) and dentists (dentophobia), fear of illness (hypochondria), germs (mysophobia), and fear of needles (trypanophobia); social phobias, spiritual phobias such as of judgment day, folklore creatures (mythophobia) and ghosts (phasmaphobia), and in recent years, nomophobia—the phobia of not having one's mobile phone resulting from an obsession to use it every minute.

An example of this difference would be having a normal fear of needles where an individual may close his eyes and squeeze a stress ball while having a blood sample drawn, while having a phobia of needles or trypanophobia would completely prevent the individual from going to a doctor for fear of being subjected to laboratory exams requiring the insertion of needles, which may ultimately lead to his death in case he has a fatal disease which was not detected due to his refusal to be examined.

To find courage in these situations, one only needs to ask himself if his fear is worth his life.

Make a stand: should one live in courage or die in fear?

Understanding One's Fear

"Fear is a question: What are you afraid of, and why? Just as the seed of health is in illness, because illness contains information, your fears are a treasure house of self-knowledge if you explore them."

– Marilyn Ferguson

Upon deciding that fear is not worth your life, one must try to overcome their fear. In order to overcome fear, the first step is to understand it. In order to understand your fear, you must identify your fear and the root cause of such fear.

Indentifying One's Fear

A person can fear many things at the same time. This may lead to future psychological disorders such as anxiety and panic disorders or even schizophrenia. Thus, it is important to know exactly what one fears in order to be able to ultimately identify and analyze the root cause of fear thus enabling a person to overcome it. This can be done by simply naming or listing down all of your fears. For instance, someone can start by recognizing that they have a fear of spiders.

The next step is to identify exactly what one fears about the certain object or situation. With respect to the example of spiders, the person shall proceed to ask themselves what exactly they fears about them. It may be their dark colors, large size, long furry legs and bodies, ability to move fast, capacity for jumping or the effects of their bites.

After identifying one's object of fear and the exact qualities which make them fearful, one may proceed to identify and analyze the root cause of his fear.

Indentifying Root Causes of Fear

The root causes of one's fear are the reasons why he fears certain objects or situations. They entail a recollection of details as to how they came to fear a certain object or situation. Through this, they will be able to focus on the proper way to handle their own fears. In general, the root causes of fear can be divided into conditioned and traumatic causes.

Conditioned Causes of Fear

Conditioned causes are those which are learned or acquired from informational sources such as reading or watching about the effects of certain situations where explicit descriptions or vivid pictures of pain are shown. In the example given on spiders, a conditioned cause may be watching a movie or television show where spiders were portrayed as threatening and dangerous creatures or seeing pictures of people suffering or dying from spider bites.

Traumatic Causes of Fear

Traumatic causes are those where an individual has suffered from a previous incident which has led him to fear the certain object or situation such as bullying, neglect, being bitten by a dog, surviving mass violence and wars, torture, natural calamities, domestic violence or maltreatment and sexual abuse. Since trauma is an emotional reaction, it is often aggravated by some circumstances surrounding the occurrence of the event which may affect one's feelings towards other things in the long run. Some of these circumstances are the unexpectedness of its occurrence, the lack of readiness on the part of the individual, the frequency of the incident, the deliberate intent in its infliction and that it occurred during childhood. They often destroy one's sense of security and accentuate one's vulnerability.

In the case of example on spiders, one may have actually suffered from a bite or has known someone who suffered or died from it.

In the United States alone, nearly three-fourths of adults or more than two hundred million individuals have experienced at least one traumatic event in their lives where around thirty million or twenty percent have developed post-traumatic stress disorders. Unfortunately, people experiencing such disorders have been found to be severely affected as they have often resorted to harmful coping mechanisms such as alcohol and drug abuse to obscure their pain. These have consequently led to aggressive behavior and decreased capacity for work and interpersonal relationships.

However, these disorders need not be experienced as long as one can face his fears and deal with them appropriately. In the end, there are only two ways of handling fear: avoiding them or facing them.

Avoiding one's fears is not necessarily an act of weakness since some fears are rational. For instance, why would one deliberately lock himself in a room full of something he fears like scorpions when he knows that there is a possible danger of being stung and dying? Avoiding exposure to harmful fears is a reasonable precaution. However, avoiding opportunities because of this fear is unreasonable. Thus, it is important to learn how to face one's fears.

The first step to overcome fear is to understand it.

Facing Fear

"What is needed, rather than running away or controlling or suppressing of any other resistance, is understanding fear; that means, watch it, learn about it, come directly into contact with it. We are to learn about fear, not how to escape from it."

– Jiddu Krishnamurti

Understanding one's fear involves more than just recognizing the reason for it. It involves facing it oneself. In order to face one's fear, one must be fully equipped as he should be before engaging in battle. He must arm himself with the proper knowledge and training before meeting his enemy. In case these prove to be insufficient, therapy or medication may also be used.

Knowledge

Learning about the object or subject of one's fear is the most important step in facing fear. This enables one to gather sufficient information on how to avoid, deal with, or even eliminate the fear. For instance, in the case of arachnophobia, knowing that there are only ten spiders which are considered as the most dangerous out of the forty thousand species that exist in the world may help him lessen his fear of spiders in general. Concentrating on the ten most dangerous species which are the brown recluse, the black widow, the Brazilian wandering spider, the Sidney funnel spider, the mouse spider, the red back spider, the wolf spider, the goliath tarantula bird-eating spider, the sac spider, and the hobo spider will enable one to recognize their appearance and pinpoint their habitat so he can prepare himself for an encounter with them in case he finds himself in their territory or finds them in his.

Training

Since training involves the use of practical skills in performing specific tasks, one must be prepared on how to handle his fears by researching on ways of eliminating them. With respect to fears related to living things such as in the example of arachnophobia, for instance, insect sprays do not usually work on spiders probably for the main reason that they are not considered as insects. Pouring seventy percent isopropyl alcohol, kerosene or anything acidic on them can damage their central nervous system and weaken them. The best way to eliminate them and ensure their death is still to whack them with a rolled up newspaper, a fly swatter or any long-handled blunt instrument that can enable one to hit them without going too near them. In this way, one is able to exercise control over the spider thus making him realize that he is more powerful than the spider thereby contributing to a decrease in his fear.

In other words, in order to overcome fear, one must always be ready with measures that would allow him to be in control of otherwise fearful events or objects. Planning ahead in terms of envisioning oneself in a fearful situation or with a fearful object may help reduce fear in the actual situation. With respect to other types of fear, one can envision himself in a plane hostage situation before his actual flight so he can think of ways of helping himself and apply them when that situation arrives. The only way to overcome fear is to be ready to face them when they surface.

Exposure

Since not all fears can be eliminated by destruction, one way of eradicating them is by actual exposure or meeting the enemy head-on. This is especially applicable to social fears, psychological fears, and harmless physical fears.

Exposure entails repeated exposure under controlled conditions. For instance, repeatedly exposing oneself to darkness may enable one to realize that nothing bad will happen in the dark thereby lessen the phobia of darkness, or constantly exposing oneself to non-venomous snakes may enable one to eliminate the fear of snakes. However, this does not mean that one should let down their defenses and be less cautious in dark environments or of venomous snakes.

Knowledge, training, and exposure are generally recommended for conditioned causes of fear. However, traumatic causes may require the professional treatment like therapy or medication.

Therapy

When one is not confident to go through the steps on their own, they may seek the help of professionals or of related interest groups through therapy. In this way, the person can develop more confidence and receive support in overcoming their fears, especially when the root cause of fear is trauma.

Yet, even without the help of a specialist, one may recover from trauma by first allowing him or herself to grieve by recalling the events or the feelings that they has been avoiding. Grief can only be known by the person feeling it. It cannot be shared by others as they can only provide sympathy. It is only by allowing oneself to grieve that they can allow themselves to heal. The process of grieving can never be hastened. It should be allowed to pass. Some people need only a short time to do so yet others spend almost their lifetime doing so.

Unless one processes the traumatic experience, it will remain in the subconscious and will continue to bother the person for a long time. Sharing the experience with others before accepting the fact that it happened is only a futile exercise, as it releases only words from one's mouth but not the emotion.

An effective way to get over trauma is to volunteer to help others face a similar situation one has gone through. Only that person can know how they can or want to be helped as a victim of a traumatic experience. By volunteering to help others and applying the method one believes would be helpful, they are also helping themselves in the process.

By doing this, he or she is able to lessen the fear he carries from the traumatic experience.

Medication

Where conscious efforts of learning, training, and exposure are not possible or when the individual is not yet ready to undergo such steps, an alternative way to eliminate fear is to use medication.

Under proper prescription, medications such as anti-depressants and other sedatives may help relieve the anxiety produced by fear. In relation to this, some studies indicate that the D-cycloserine antibiotic used in the treatment of tuberculosis may help eliminate fear together with therapies to erase memories associated with fear. However, one cannot disregard some side-effects that may be produced with prolonged use.

Thus, it is better to exert greater effort in helping oneself overcome his fears than relying on substances.

The best way to understand fear is to face it.

Overcoming Fear

"Courage is not the absence of fear, but rather the judgment that something else is more important than fear."

– Ambrose Redmoon

In order to ultimately overcome fear or at least, act in spite of it, one must find a reason to do so—a reason that weighs more than the fear itself.

As there are different types of fear, so are there different types of courage which can generally be classified according to the reasons which induce a person to exercise them—physical courage, emotional courage, moral courage, and rational courage.

In other words, each type of courage is associated with the type of fear it stems from. Thus, physical courage is an outcome of physical fear such as losing one's life in an attack; emotional courage is a result of the emotional fear of having to deal with unpleasant experiences in life; moral courage is present when an act is done in spite of the fear of the consequence of making a moral choice; and rational courage arises from the fear of the effects of the use of reasoning.

However, it is the decision to act for a value greater than that which is feared makes the exercise of courage possible. For instance, if a person values his own life more than his fear of losing it, he will protect it at all costs thereby exercising physical courage; if a person values his own happiness more than his fear of sadness he will exercise emotional courage by finding ways to experience happiness in spite of sadness; if a person values justice more than the rule of majority, he will exercise moral courage by fighting for it in spite of possible isolation; and if one values efficiency resulting from new methods more than his fear of being ridiculed for non-adherence to traditional practices, he will exercise rational courage by espousing his ideas.

Yet in all courageous acts, judgment must be used.

An act of courage is a conscious choice. As in all types of decision-making, there must be a greater motive involved.

Boosting Physical Courage

"Courage is almost a contradiction in terms. It means a strong desire to live taking the form of a readiness to die."

– G. K. Chesterton

Physical courage is often associated with typical acts of valor and honor of soldiers in wars. It generally indicates bravery in the face of physical harm or even the threat of death. In modern times, it is simply and commonly known as acting in self-defense or in defense of another.

In order to boost physical courage, one only has to put a greater value on his life or on the life of another in order to enable him to reach the maximum level where he is prepared to die so that he or another may live. This may involve thinking of the welfare of those who are dependent on him or on the other person, his personal goals or ambitions which he feels he must achieve in his lifetime or the significance of the other person in his life.

Yet, the ultimate desired result of this endeavor is to endure and triumph in the end.

In order to live, one must be ready to die.

Fostering Emotional Courage

"We are biological creatures. We are born, we live, we die. There is no transcendent purpose to existence. At best we are creatures of reason, and by using reason we can cure ourselves of emotional excess. Purged of both hope and fear, we find courage in the face of helplessness, insignificance and uncertainty."

– Jonathan Sacks

Contrary to its connotation, emotional courage does not mean expressing emotions openly regardless of the consequences. On the other hand, it involves one's openness to undergo all emotional experiences, whether positive or negative without destroying oneself in the process. As such, it requires applying the Aristotelian philosophy of choosing the middle of two extremes in order to rid oneself of emotional excesses for it is only then that one will be able to survive the emotional vicissitudes in life.

Fostering emotional courage entails accepting the reality that there will always be changes which may cause pleasant or unpleasant experiences. In doing so, one subconsciously prepares himself for the possibility of the occurrence of an unfavorable event thereby decreasing the negative impact it would have on his feelings when it arises.

Then we can say that we are ready to face life with courage.

Emotional courage is not about the denial of one's feelings. Rather, it is about tempering them.

Developing Moral Courage

"A man does what he must—in spite of personal consequences, in spite of obstacles and dangers and pressures—and that is the basis of all human morality."

– John F. Kennedy

Moral courage involves recognizing the existence of a moral situation and acting in accordance with one's moral principles or values and therefore making a moral choice. It therefore consists in doing what is right in spite of the inconvenience it may cause in one's life such as rejection, ridicule, or even isolation.

An example of this was shown by Yu Panglin, a Chinese realty and hotel magnate who, instead of leaving his sons his money as rich Chinese families would, donated his last $470 million to his charitable institutions because he was aware of the sufferings and hardships of the poor in his country. For common people, it involves making moral choices in daily activities where questions of morality may arise such as disclosing unethical or illegal business practices even if it means earning the resentment of co-workers or reporting prohibited acts such as cheating in spite of the possible ridicule from fellow students.

In order to encourage moral courage, one only has to consult his conscience.

An act of moral courage is an act of conscience.

Intensifying Rational Courage

"True courage is a result of reasoning. A brave mind is always impregnable."

– Jeremy Collier

Rational courage involves the use of reason to achieve any of these three things: discovering and promoting new ideas as well as discerning and conveying the truth, questioning one's beliefs, and thinking and overcoming one's own problems. Hence, there are three types of rational courage: intellectual, philosophical, and psychological.

Encouraging Intellectual Courage

Intellectual courage involves one's willingness to discover and promote new ideas as well as to discern and convey the truth. It also entails one's openness to take the risk of making mistakes, failing, or even being ridiculed as Copernicus (for his heliocentric theory of the universe), Gregor Mendel (for his laws of inheritance), and Albert Einstein (for his theory of relativity) have experienced in their exercise of intellectual courage.

Nevertheless, it is because of this type of courage that inventions and innovations have materialized—the benefits of which are enjoyed at present.

After all, as Albert Einstein himself once said, "What is right is not always popular and what is popular is not always right."

In order to encourage intellectual courage, one must always endeavor to seek the truth that it may be found.

Strengthening Philosophical Courage

Philosophical courage varies from the other types of courage in that it is a matter of extent more than a decision to act. In other words, courage is determined by how far one is willing to question his fundamental principles and beliefs. The farther one goes in his level of questioning, the greater philosophical courage he has. For instance, if a man is willing to question his beliefs, which he once considered unquestionable, then he is exercising a high degree of philosophical courage.

While this type of courage also entails the acceptance of the possibility of obtaining no definite answers, it nevertheless allows one to be free from biases as it broadens one's views which will eventually enable him to practice critical thinking and secure his freedom. For instance, unless one challenges his views about the existence of a god as well as his own religion, his thoughts and decisions will always be clouded by his religious beliefs which may cause his eternal slavery and hamper his development. For instance, the Catholic religion rejects the use of contraceptives as a means of birth control, and in some extreme cases, rejects birth control itself which will cause a person—particularly the woman—to be enslaved in her own body if she does not challenge or question not only this particular practice but the authority and basis upon which this belief rests as well.

However, strengthening philosophical courage entails one's willingness to let go. As T. S. Eliot writes, "Only those who risk going too far can possibly find out how far one can go." And then someday he can be free.

Improving Psychological Courage

Finally, psychological courage involves one's ability to overcome a crisis, particularly that of a diagnosed psychological problem such as a destructive or harmful habit or an unfounded anxiety. It mainly involves one's desire to reach a resolution himself as only he can direct his mind towards that which he wishes to achieve.

Improving psychological courage entails acknowledging the existence of a psychological problem. It is only then that one can move to help himself. In the words of Aristotle himself, "I count him braver who overcomes his desires than him who conquers his enemies; for the hardest victory is over self."

True courage comes with a free mind.

How to Apply Key Ideas for the Best Results?

How fear affects one's life is a matter of choice. Fear clouds the mind. Having a clear mind requires getting rid of one's fears. Getting rid of one's fears is possible only if one knows what they are.

Make a stand: should one live in courage or die in fear? The first step to overcome fear is to understand it. The best way to understand fear is to face it.

An act of courage is a conscious choice. As in all types of decision-making, there must be a greater motive involved. In order to live, one must be ready to die.

Emotional courage is not about the denial of one's feelings. Rather, it is about tempering them.

An act of moral courage is an act of conscience.

True courage comes with a free mind.

www.ingramcontent.com/pod-product-compliance
Lightning Source LLC
Chambersburg PA
CBHW070423190526
45169CB00003B/1382